Contents

What are boats?

Boats are **vehicles** that float on water.

They can carry people or things.

engine

Many boats have **engines** or motors to push them through the water.

People or wind can make boats move, too.

What do boats look like?

bow

Many boats are large and long.

Their **bows** come to a point at the front.

Some boats are small and short.

Boats can be any colour.

What are boats made of?

engine

The outsides of many boats are metal or wood.

The **engines** are made of metal.

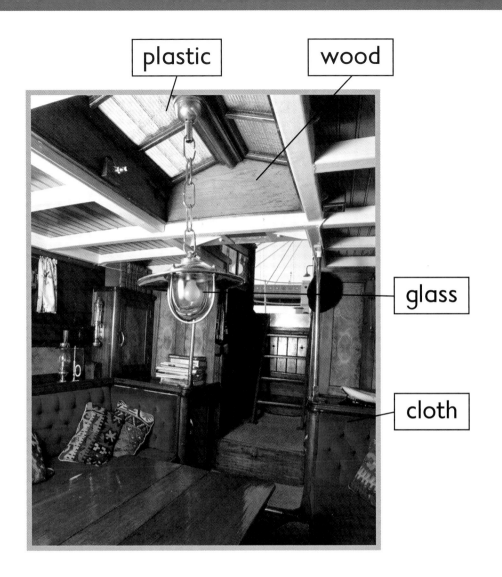

plastic

wood

glass

cloth

The insides of boats are made of wood and cloth.

Some parts are made of glass or plastic.

How did boats look in the past?

raft

The first boats were rafts made of tree trunks tied together.

Some people still use rafts today.

wheel

Later, paddle boats carried many people.

A big turning wheel at the back or side of the boat pushed it forward.

What is a rowing boat?

oar

Rowing boats are small boats without **engines**.

People use **oars** to pull the boat through water.

Some people go rowing for fun.

Some people use rowing boats to go fishing.

What is a sailing boat?

sail

Sailing boats have big cloth sails.

The sails catch the wind and push the boat.

sails

Some sailing boats only hold one person.

Large sailing boats can hold many people.

What is a motorboat?

engine

Motorboats are boats with small **engines** that push them across the water.

Motorboats can pull people on **inner tubes**.

Some people ride on **water skis** behind motorboats.

What is a ferry?

A ferry is a boat that carries **passengers** on short journeys.

People can drive their cars on to some ferries.

Other ferries only carry people.

This ferry is taking passengers on a day out to see interesting things.

Why are some boats special?

Submarines are boats that can dive deep underwater.

Scientists can study the ocean from a submarine.

Fireboats pump water.

They can put out fires on boats at sea.

Quiz

Do you know what kind of boat this is?

Can you find it in the book?

Look for the answer on page 24.

Glossary

bow
name for the front part of a boat

engine
machine that makes a vehicle move

inner tube
air-filled tube inside a tyre that floats

oar
long pole used to push a boat through the water

passengers
people who travel from one place to another in a vehicle

vehicle
machine that carries people or things from place to place

water skis
long, thin pieces of plastic or wood worn on the feet used to move across water

Index

Answer to quiz on page 22.
This is a sailing boat.

24

Titles in the Wheels, Wings and Water series include:

Hardback   1 844 21369 2

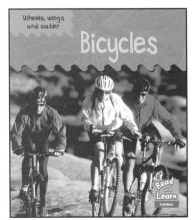

Hardback   1 844 21371 4

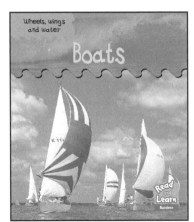

Hardback   1 844 21366 8

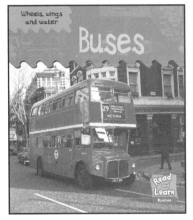

Hardback   1 844 21373 0

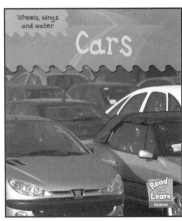

Hardback   1 844 21372 2

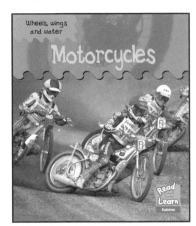

Hardback   1 844 21367 6

Hardback   1 844 21368 4

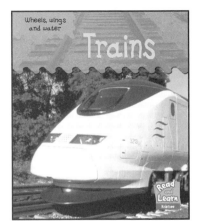

Hardback   1 844 21374 9

Find out about the other titles in this series on our website www.raintreepublishers.co.uk

PUFFIN BOOKS

Published by the Penguin Group
Penguin Books Ltd, 80 Strand, London WC2R 0RL, England
Penguin Putnam Inc., 375 Hudson Street, New York, New York 10014, USA
Penguin Books Australia Ltd, 250 Camberwell Road, Camberwell, Victoria 3124, Australia
Penguin Books Canada Ltd, 10 Alcorn Avenue, Toronto, Ontario, Canada M4V 3B2
Penguin Books India (P) Ltd, 11 Community Centre, Panchsheel Park, New Delhi – 110 017, India
Penguin Books (NZ) Ltd, Cnr Rosedale and Airborne Roads, Albany, Auckland, New Zealand
Penguin Books (South Africa) (Pty) Ltd, 24 Sturdee Avenue, Rosebank 2196, South Africa

Penguin Books Ltd, Registered Offices: 80 Strand, London WC2R 0RL, England

www.penguin.com

First published 2002
1 3 5 7 9 10 8 6 4 2

Printed at Oriental Press, Dubai, U.A.E.

British Library Cataloguing in Publication Data
A CIP catalogue record for this book is available from the British Library

ISBN 0–670–89421–4

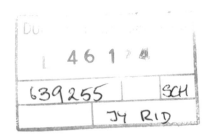

Platypus

CHRIS RIDDELL

and the
Lucky
Day

PUFFIN BOOKS

Platypus found a banana he had forgotten about under his pillow. "Today must be my lucky day," he said, jumping out of bed.

"Today is a perfect day for kite flying," said Platypus.

But the string on his kite was tangled up.

"Lucky I have some spare string in my collecting box," he said.

Platypus went
outside to
fly his kite.

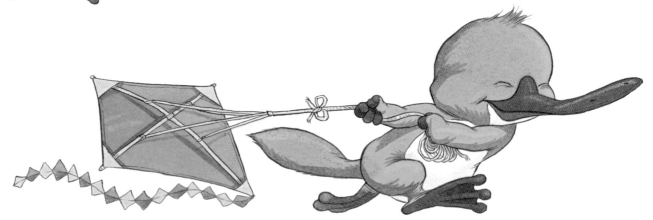

It was very windy
but he held on
tight until . . .

... SNAP! The string broke.

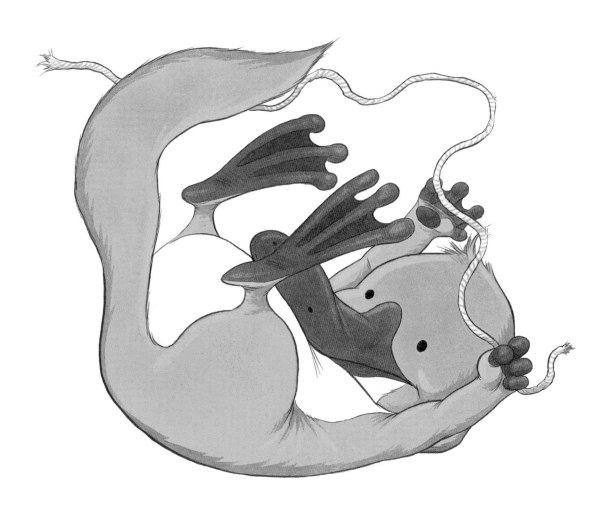

"Lucky that tree was there to catch my kite,"
said Platypus looking up into the branches.

He started to climb the tree. His fingertips could just touch the kite but . . .

... CRACK! The branch broke.

"What a perfect day for painting pictures," said Platypus.

He got out his paints and his painting apron.

Platypus painted a beautiful picture, but just as he was colouring in the sky . . .

… there was a sudden gust of wind.

"Oh no!" said Platypus.
"Lucky I was wearing
my apron."

But his lovely
painting was ruined.

Then it began to rain,

very hard.

Platypus ran indoors.

He tripped up on the old kite string
and bumped his head.

"I was wrong," sniffed Platypus sadly. "Today is not my lucky day."

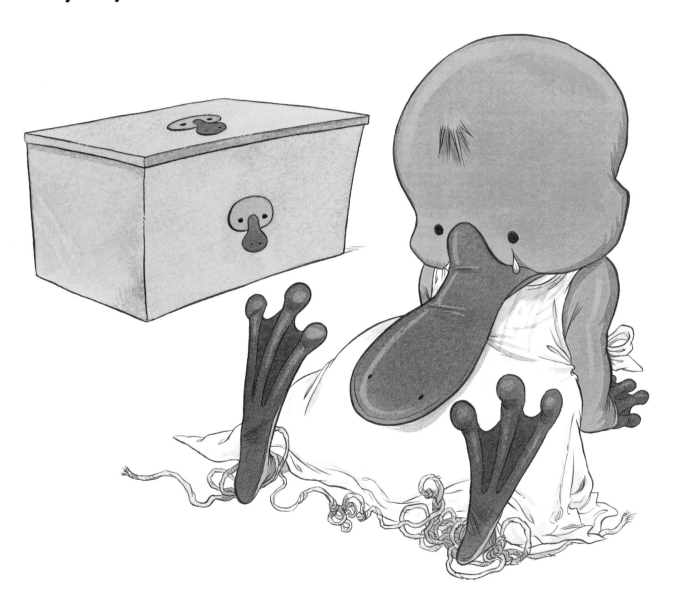

"I'm going back to bed!" he said.

Platypus found the banana he'd forgotten about under his pillow. He ate it and began to feel a little better.

He found Bruce too, under the duvet.

"I thought I'd lost you!" he said, hugging Bruce.
He began to feel a lot better.

Outside, it was still raining. "What a perfect day for tidying my cupboard," said Platypus.

He found all sorts of things
he'd forgotten about,

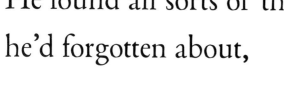

or tidied away,

or thought were
broken . . .

. . . but found he could mend.

Best of all, Platypus found his special hat.

The rain stopped and the sun came out. "What a perfect day for go-carting!" said Platypus running outside. He climbed to the top of the hill.

"Whee!" he laughed, whizzing down the hill. His hat slipped over his eyes and he couldn't see where he was going.

BUMP! Platypus crashed into a tree.

Something landed in his lap. "My kite!"
said Platypus excitedly. "This is
my lucky day after all."